D1383817

American History Arts & Crafts

LEARNING ABOUT
COLONIAL AMERICA

WITH ARTS & CRAFTS

Paul Challen

PowerKiDS press

New York

Published in 2015 by **The Rosen Publishing Group, Inc.**
29 East 21st Street, New York, NY 10010

Library of Congress Cataloging-in-Publication-Data

Challen, Paul C. (Paul Clarence), 1967-
 Learning about Colonial America with arts & crafts / Paul Challen.
    pages cm. — (American history arts & crafts)
 Includes index.
ISBN 978-1-4777-5834-2 (pbk.)
ISBN 978-1-4777-5747-5 (6 pack)
ISBN 978-1-4777-5836-6 (library binding)
1. United States—History—Colonial period, ca. 1600-1775—Juvenile literature.
2. United States—History—Colonial period, ca. 1600-1775—Study and teaching—Activity
programs—Juvenile literature. I. Title. II. Title: Learning about Colonial America with arts and crafts.
 E188.C39 2015
 973.2—dc23

                          2014033930

Developed and produced for Rosen by BlueAppleWorks Inc.
Art Director: T. J. Choleva
Managing Editor for BlueAppleWorks: Melissa McClellan
Photo Research: Jane Reid
Editor: Marcia Abramson
Craft Consultant: Jerrie McClellan

Photo & Illustration Credits:
Cover, p. 13 bottom, 14 Jean Leon Gerome Ferris/Library of Congress/Public Domain; cover side images (top, title page,
p. 10 left Shaiith/Shutterstock; middle, p. 18 left Bobby Deal/Dreamstime; bottom, p. 22 left Photowitch/Dreamstime);
p. 4 right RCPPhoto/Shutterstock; sidebars Dariusz Pawlowski/Shutterstock; maps p. 4, 8, 15, 24 T. J. Choleva; p. 5
Public Domain; p. 6 John Gadsby Chapman/Architect of the Capitol/Public Domain; p. 7 left, p. 12 bottom, 13 top, 16
top, 27 bottom National Park Service, Colonial National Historical Park, Jamestown Collection; p. 7 right William M. S.
Rasmussen/Public Domain; p. 8 top William Halsall/Public Domain; p. 8 Alfred Walter Bayes/Public Domain; p. 9 left Bill
Price III/Creative Commons; p. 9 right W. Endicott & Co./Library of Congress/Public Domain; p. 10–11, 18–19, 22–23,
28–29 Austen Photography; p. 12 top The German Kali Works/Public Domain; p. 15 top Tomas Skopal/Shutterstock;
p. 15 bottom John Wolcott Adams and I.N. Phelps Stokes/Public Domain; p. 16–17 bottom Carlyn Iverson; p. 17 top right
The Hugh C. Leighton Company/Public Domain; p. 17 bottom right Thomas Birch/Public Domain; p. 20 T. J. Choleva (Eric
Isselee/Shutterstock, Anthonycz/Shutterstock, Americanspirit/Dreamstime); p. 21 left Caspar Netscher/Public Domain;
p. 21 right Public Domain; p. 22 top Wavebreakmedia Ltd/Dreamstime; p. 24 bottom Jim David/Shutterstock; p. 24 top
A.S. Seer Print/Library of Congress/Public Domain; p. 25 top The Library of Virginia/Public Domain; p. 25 bottom Eyre
Crowe/Public Domain; p. 26 top Lori Martin/Shutterstock; p. 26 William Aiken Walker/Public Domain; p. 27 top Public
Domain; p. 28 left Rukodelnica/Dreamstime; p. 28 top Lizapolina/Dreamstime

Manufactured in the United States of America
CPSIA Compliance Information: Batch #CW15PK For Further Information contact: Rosen Publishing, New York, New York at 1-800-237-9932

Table of Contents

The Thirteen Colonies

When we talk about the history of colonial America today, we are talking about the original thirteen English **colonies** that made up what would later become the United States.

The colonies grew very quickly. In 1700, there were about 250,000 European settlers there. Just before the American Revolution began, 75 years later, there were ten times as many. Although these **colonists** seemed not to have a lot in common, they were able to band together to win their independence from England.

The colonists sailed to America in large, crowded ships.

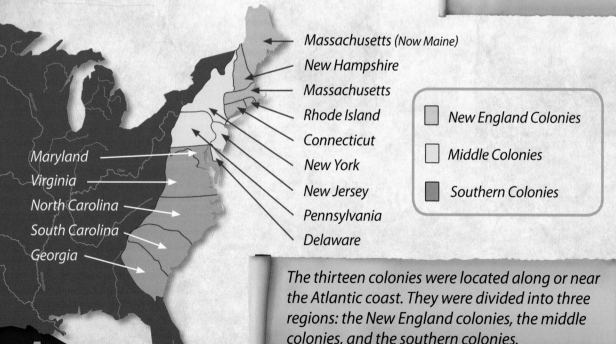

Massachusetts (Now Maine)
New Hampshire
Massachusetts
Rhode Island
Connecticut
New York
New Jersey
Pennsylvania
Delaware

Maryland
Virginia
North Carolina
South Carolina
Georgia

■ New England Colonies
□ Middle Colonies
■ Southern Colonies

The thirteen colonies were located along or near the Atlantic coast. They were divided into three regions: the New England colonies, the middle colonies, and the southern colonies.

People in the Colonies

Although people from England claimed these areas in the name of their monarch, settlers had been coming from places like Spain, France, and the Netherlands before the arrival of the British. Of course, many **Native Americans** had also lived in these regions for many generations.

People came from Europe to the colonies for many reasons. Some wanted to come to an area where they would be free to practice their religion, own land, or build a better life—all things they found impossible in their homeland. Others were attracted by tales of adventure they had heard about life in the new land. Unfortunately, many others of African descent were brought to the colonies as **slaves** who had no rights or freedom. They were bought and sold for their labor.

INDENTURED SERVANTS

One group of people who arrived in the colonies were **indentured servants**. These were people who came to work based on a contract. This system was especially used as a way for poor English people to get passage to the American colonies. They would work for a fixed number of years, then be free to work on their own. Some worked as farmers or helpers for farm wives; some were apprenticed to craftsmen.

Many people were captured in Africa and brought to America on slave ships.

Jamestown Colony

The first permanent colony was established in Jamestown in Virginia. It was named after King James I and historians set its founding at 1607, the year that English people arrived there.

The people who settled Jamestown came mostly from England. Because of climate there, these early colonists were optimistic that they could make Jamestown a success. Their early years, though, were very difficult. For example, during the winter of 1609-10, known as the "Starving Time," only 60 of the 500 colonists who lived there survived due to starvation and poor drinking water.

However, when the Englishman John Rolfe arrived in Jamestown in 1610, he brought a special type of **tobacco** seeds with him. The soil and growing conditions in coastal Virginia proved to be ideal for growing this type of tobacco, and because the colonists were able to grow it and sell it successfully, their settlement started to grow.

John Rolfe was one of the most important early English settlers of North America.

Roanoke – The "Lost Colony"

About 25 years before the founding of Jamestown, explorers from England also tried to set up a colony in Roanoke, North Carolina. The settlers had a lot of difficulty establishing the colony, and the last of the surviving colonists disappeared during the Anglo-Spanish War of 1585-1604. To this day, nobody can say for certain what happened to the Roanoke colonists. The experiences of the "Lost Colony" are important because they show that establishing a successful colony was actually very difficult.

JOHN ROLFE AND POCAHONTAS

John Rolfe made the voyage from England to the New World with his wife, Sarah Hacker. Sarah died during the time their ship was landed in Bermuda. Upon his arrival in Virginia, Rolfe met and eventually married the Native American Pocahontas. Their marriage was seen as a strong force for keeping harmony between the Native Americans and the colonists.

John Rolfe married Pocahontas, daughter of the local Native American leader Powhatan, in 1614.

Early colonists built the walls of the fort at Jamestown.

7

The New England Colonies and the Pilgrims

The first colonists to arrive in the New England states are known as the **Pilgrims**. The first of these people came on the famous ship *Mayflower*, which left England in August of 1620, and arrived at Cape Cod in Massachusetts in November.

The Mayflower *was the ship that transported Pilgrims from Plymouth in England to North America.*

The Massachusetts Bay Colony was founded in 1630. Its founders were **Puritans**, members of a religious group that found it difficult to observe their faith in their homeland.

The New England Colonies

Massachusetts (Now Maine)

New Hampshire

Massachusetts

Rhode Island

Connecticut

Puritans left Europe and traveled to America where they could practice their religion without restrictions.

Spreading Out

After settling in Massachusetts, more Puritans arrived, settling in Connecticut, New Hampshire, and Rhode Island. The Puritans lived very strict religious lives and not all of the colonists liked their rules. One of the most famous of these colonists was Roger Williams. He spoke against the strict rules of the community and for that was expelled from the Massachusetts colony. After that Roger Williams founded the Rhode Island colony in 1636. Williams thought that it was important to set up a colony where people of all faiths could worship freely.

DID YOU KNOW?

The Puritans took schooling very seriously. They wanted their children to be well-versed in the Bible, and also prized writing and penmanship very highly. These colonists thought so highly of education that Massachusetts created the colonies' first public school system. As part of this system and due to a law passed in 1647, every town had to have at least one schoolteacher, paid through the contributions of every citizen.

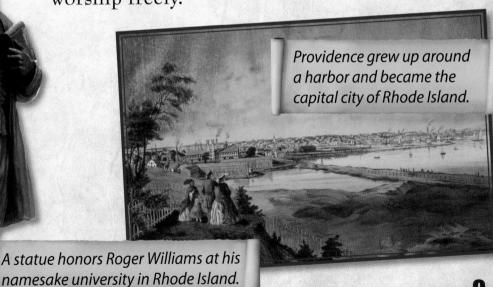

Providence grew up around a harbor and became the capital city of Rhode Island.

A statue honors Roger Williams at his namesake university in Rhode Island.

Craft to Make:

Quill Pen and Ink

The written word was the most important way the colonists had of keeping in touch with friends and family back home and was a key part of doing business in their new land. Most pens at the time were made from bird feathers. These pens could be hard to find and expensive, so most colonists made their own.

Writing was a valuable skill in colonial times.

What You Will Need

- Large feathers (available at most craft stores)
- Scissors
- Water
- Small bottle
- Food coloring
- Paper

Step One

Select a large feather with a hollow center. With the scissors, cut the tip of the feather (the "quill") at a diagonal angle. Remove any extra quill from the end so your diagonal cut is nice and clean. Then cut a small vertical slit up into the tip of the pen. This will help the feather draw up and hold the ink for writing.

Step Two

Pour a small amount of water into your bowl or bottle. Add food coloring to the water, a few drops at a time. The more coloring you add, the darker your "ink" will be.

Step Three

Dip the end of your quill pen into the ink and begin writing! The thicker your paper, the better able it will be to absorb your ink. You'll have to re-dip every few letters.

Native Americans and Colonists

Squanto was the Native American who showed the Pilgrims how to fertilize their crops with dead fish.

Of course, English and other colonists were not the first humans to set foot in the so-called "New World." Native Americans had been there many centuries before and had established themselves as experts in knowing how to hunt animals for food and clothing and in growing crops to eat.

When the colonists arrived, many Native American tribes taught them valuable lessons about hunting, trapping, fishing, and farming. They also passed on important knowledge about how to survive the winter, which in New England especially was very harsh.

The colonists traded goods with Native Americans.

Thanksgiving and Conflict

Most Americans know the story of the first Thanksgiving, in which the Pilgrims and Native Americans in Massachusetts joined together to celebrate a successful fall harvest and a life of harmony together.

However, many colonists and native people did not get along so well. Colonial history also contains many instances of fighting between the two groups, as natives resisted the attempts of settlers to take over the land they had always considered as theirs.

Native Americans and Pilgrim settlers celebrated together at the first Thanksgiving.

The Middle Colonies

Below the New England colonies, another set of colonies emerged. Because of their location, they are known as the middle colonies, made up of New York, Pennsylvania, New Jersey, and Delaware.

Pennsylvania got its name from William Penn, the founder of the colony. Its name tells us something about the early landscape of the colony, because "Pennsylvania" is a combination of Penn's name and the Latin word for "forest" (*sylvania*). So the name means "Penn's forest." In time, that colony would be the home of one of America's most important cities, Philadelphia.

William Penn first landed at the territory of Pennsylvania in 1682.

Life in the Middle Colonies

Because they had similar climates and landscape, the middle colonies developed very similarly to the colonies of New England. Farming was particularly important as farmers both ate and sold their crops. Many small towns grew in these colonies to eventually become big cities. Indeed, the largest city in the United States today, New York City, started life as a Dutch settlement called New Amsterdam, founded in 1625.

The Middle Colonies

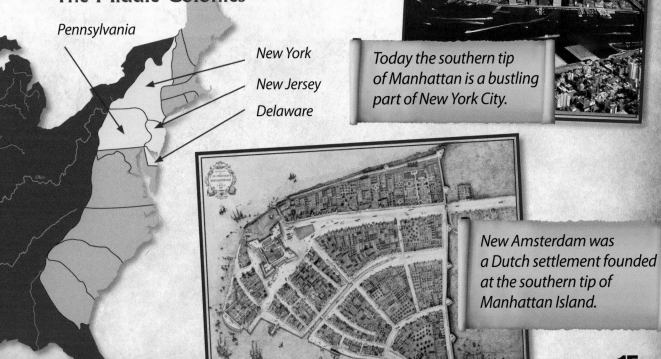

Pennsylvania

New York

New Jersey

Delaware

Today the southern tip of Manhattan is a bustling part of New York City.

New Amsterdam was a Dutch settlement founded at the southern tip of Manhattan Island.

15

Towns and Villages

As more and more settlers arrived in the colonies, the population also grew as colonists began having families. With this growth in population, people realized that joining together to live in towns and villages made a lot of sense, because it allowed people to live and work closely together to achieve common aims.

For example, village stores gave people a place to go to buy the things they needed to maintain their homes. Churches allowed them to come together to worship. Streets and squares provided places to meet with townspeople to share news.

Colonial towns housed many artisans, shopkeepers, and merchants who provided services to the growing farming population.

Home Building

Colonists made good use of their resources to build their homes. In the middle colonies, trees were often cut down to make planks for building houses. Dutch colonists often used entire logs to build theirs, and the "log cabin" design became popular as Americans started spreading west. German and Welsh settlers in Pennsylvania followed the way of their homeland and built their houses entirely of stone.

Colonists cut down trees to clear land for farming, then used the wood for building.

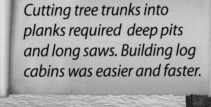

Cutting tree trunks into planks required deep pits and long saws. Building log cabins was easier and faster.

17

Craft to Make:

Dipped Candles

Inside the homes, churches, and workplaces of the colonists, there was a constant need for light. Without electricity and with glass windows being rare (and small even when they did exist), a cheap, easy source of light was crucial.

Colonists knew how to burn whale oil as a source of light (see page 21), but this was hard to get and expensive. Instead, they became experts at making simple "dipped" candles. These candles were made of wax. They provided a great source of light for reading, cooking, or doing other activities indoors.

With a little practice, you can make a dipped candle just like the colonists did!

What You Will Need

- Wax
- Empty washed can
- Pot of water
- Spoon for stirring
- Crayons
- Scissors
- Candlewick or string
- Pencil

(Note: You will need an adult's help to do this craft!)

Step One

Cut or break the wax into small pieces (about the size of a sugar cube). With an adult's help, put the wax in your can and put the can into a pot of water. Set the heat to medium. Stir the pieces of wax slowly as they melt. If you want to add color, add a small piece of crayon after removing the paper wrapper. When the wax is completely liquid, take it off the stove. (If the wax starts to harden when you are working, put it back on the stove to warm it up.)

Step Two

Cut your wick to the size of the candle you want to make. Wrap the wick over a pencil and carefully dip it into the hot wax. As you dip, the wax will stick to the wick. Lift the dipped wick out, and let it cool and harden. Repeat the dipping and cooling process over and over, as your wick takes on more and more wax.

Step Three

When your candle is as thick as you'd like, let the candle cool completely. When the candle is cooled, trim the wick to the length you want. To use the candle, ask an adult to help you put it in a candleholder and light the wick.

A Day at Work

When the colonists arrived, they wanted to recreate many of the patterns of life they had been used to in their homeland. Because their new homes had never been settled by Europeans, they had a lot of work to do.

To get food, colonists hunted animals, such as deer, turkeys, and pheasant, and grew crops such as maize (corn), beans, and potatoes. Farmers also raised animals such as horses, cows, pigs, and goats.

Colonists based their farming methods on homeland traditions. For example, German farmers preferred oxen rather than horses to pull their plows, and Scots-Irish colonists based their farming on hogs and corn.

Making Everything

The carpenter was an important person in any colonial settlement, because building homes, furniture, and other useful objects out of wood was crucial. Along with the carpenter, the blacksmith also played a vital role, because he was the one who made nails and other iron products such as horseshoes.

Colonists wore clothing such as broad hats, large buckles on pants and breeches for men, and long dresses and bonnets for women. Tailors were an important part of a community for people who could afford a tailor's services. For the most part, colonists made their clothes themselves.

WHALING

During the colonial era, whales were plentiful along the Atlantic coasts of such areas as Long Island, New York, and Massachusetts. Men called "whalers" went to sea in large boats to try to catch them, but this could be a very dangerous occupation, as whales as long as 50 feet (15.2 meters) and weighing up to 77,000 pounds (35 metric tons) would put up a tremendous fight. The whales were highly prized for their meat and their fat, which was boiled down to make oil for heat and light.

*American **whaling** originated in New York, New England, Massachusetts and nearby cities.*

Most women were highly skilled in cloth-making.

Craft to Make:

Colonial Bonnet

Because the colonists relied so much on homemade clothes, sewing skills were very important for young girls and women in the colonies.

One of the many things they made were bonnets. These cloth hats gave protection from the sun and weather. During colonial times, many people believed that women and girls should keep their hair covered, both for safety while working and for modesty.

A soft bonnet also was called a mobcap during colonial times.

What You Will Need

- Fabric square 18 inches (45.7 cm) on each side
- Pencil
- Measuring tape or ruler
- Ribbon
- Scissors

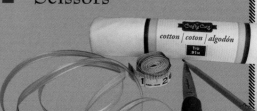

Step One

Fold your fabric from top to bottom and side to side to find the center. Make a small mark with a pencil in the center. Mark a spot 9 inches (22.9 cm) from the center with the measuring tape and pencil. Using a ruler or measuring tape, make more small marks 9 inches (22.9 cm) from the center until you have a circle. Make another series of marks 7 inches (17.8 cm) from the center, 1 inch (2.5 cm) apart.

Step Two

Following the outer marks cut out a circle from the fabric. Finish the edge of the mob cap with clear glue around the outside edge to keep the edges smooth. Using scissors, make a small cut in the fabric on the inside marks.

Step Three

Measure and cut a 36-inch (91.4 cm) piece of ribbon. Thread the ribbon through the slits you cut. Place the mobcap on your head, and slowly pull on both ends of the ribbon. Then tie the ribbon in a bow and trim the ends so they are even.

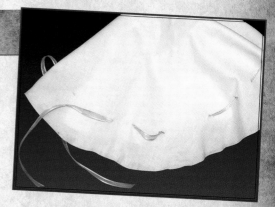

The Southern Colonies

Life in the southern colonies of Maryland, Virginia, North Carolina, South Carolina, and Georgia was very different than in the other colonies. In the South, life revolved mostly around single-crop farming, namely tobacco, rice, indigo, and **cotton**. Planting, growing, and harvesting these crops took a lot of work, and depended on a workforce that was huge and cheap.

More and more, slave labor came to be used in the southern colonies. Not all farmers owned slaves, but over time, richer farmers, known as "planters," bought large numbers of African slaves to work on their **plantations**.

The Southern Colonies

Slaves worked in the cotton fields of the southern colonies.

Maryland

Virginia

North Carolina

South Carolina

Georgia

Harvesting and cleaning cotton required many workers before machinery was invented to speed up the process.

Slavery

Slavery had existed in many parts of the world for many centuries. It was based on the idea of "forced labor." That is, slaves did not have any choice about the work they did, nor did they have any of the basic human rights such as the right to vote, marry, or express themselves that we are used to today. Although treatment of slaves by planters varied widely, it is important to remember that a slave could be bought or sold by an owner at any time

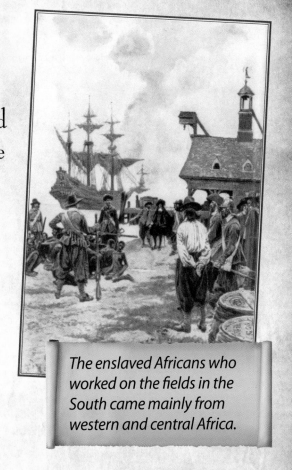

The enslaved Africans who worked on the fields in the South came mainly from western and central Africa.

Not all slaves worked in the fields. Some of them were sold and bought to work as domestic servants.

25

Plantation Life

Planters developed enormous farms known as plantations, where much more than farming took place. Cotton plantations were the most common, especially in Georgia, the Carolinas, and southern Virginia. In addition to fields of crops, plantations contained rough log or frame living quarters for slaves and other workers, barns and pens for animals, horse stables, carriage houses, roads, pathways, fences, and many other things. Planters and their families lived in a large mansion known as the **"big house."**

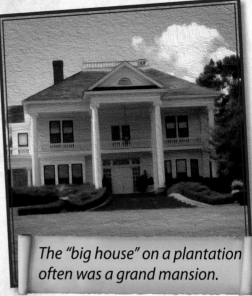

The "big house" on a plantation often was a grand mansion.

Southern plantations were often self-sufficient settlements owned by a planter. They included everything from the "big house" to the pens for livestock.

Crops for Trade

Facilities for processing the crops, such as curing tobacco or cleaning cotton seeds, could also be found on the plantation. A blacksmith shop and houses for spinning, weaving, smoking meat, and storing ice were part of a plantation too.

Slaves cured, or dried, leaves of tobacco.

These plantations generated a great deal of the agricultural output of the colonies for local use and trade. Trade with the other colonies, as well as England and Bermuda, made many planters very rich.

Much of a plantation's crop was shipped overseas and sold for a big profit.

Paper Quilling

As they built their homes, colonists in the South and in all areas enjoyed making the interiors look good with decorations. One of the most popular crafts in colonial times was paper quilling.

Paper quilling is an art form that involves being creative with paper by cutting it, rolling it, curling it, and making it into shapes. The shapes then are glued to make all kinds of designs, which can be used to decorate many different things.

These paper shapes can be used to decorate all kinds of things.

What You Will Need

- Paper (variety of colors)
- Pencil or Q-tip
- Scissors
- Clear glue

Step One

Cut strips of paper 1/8-inch (3 mm), 1/4-inch (6 mm) or 1/2 inch (12 mm) wide. To do this, make marks on your paper on the top and bottom at intervals of every width you decide on. Then draw lines between the two marks, and using your scissors, cut your strips.

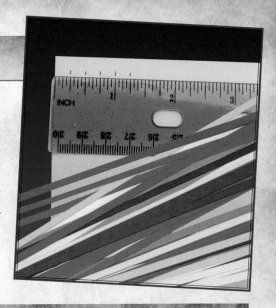

Step Two

Roll the paper onto the end of a pencil (make sure the pencil has no ridges) or Q-tip (cut one end off if using a Q-tip). When you get to the end, let go of the coil a little to loosen it, and then roll it off the object you were using. You can keep it tight or unwind a bit to a looser shape. Glue the end to the other part of the coil to keep it from unraveling.

Step Three

There are many shapes you can make from the coils by pinching the ends or unraveling part of the coil. Arrange your coils on a piece of paper and then glue each coil in place by putting a small amount of glue on one edge. The only limit to this craft is your imagination!

Glossary

big house The name given to the large plantation mansion where the planter and his family lived, along with servants.

colonist Someone who lives in a colony.

colony A geographic area that is under the control of people in another area, usually far away.

cotton A plant common in the southern colonies that produces a white, fluffy fiber that is useful for making clothes and other items out of cloth.

indentured servant A worker who is employed under a legal contract. In colonial times, these contracts had folds, or "indentures," in the middle.

Mayflower The English ship that brought Pilgrims to Plymouth Colony in 1620.

Native American The first group of inhabitants of North America who were present in the colonies when Europeans arrived.

Pilgrim The common name for the settlers of Plymouth Colony.

plantation A large agricultural area that contains fields for crops, as well as all the buildings and services needed to maintain harvesting, processing of crops, and trading.

Puritans The group of English colonists who founded Massachusetts Bay Colony in 1630 so they would have a place to practice their religion freely.

slave A person who works in conditions where he or she is not free.

tobacco A plant common in the southern colonies that can be cured (dried) and processed for use in cigarettes, cigars, etc.

whaling The hunt for whales in the ocean off the New England colonies. Whale fat was used to make oil, which was burned for heat and light.

For More Information

Further Reading

Lassieur, Allison. *Colonial America: An Interactive History Adventure.* Capstone Press, 2013.

Maestro, Betsy. *The New Americans: Colonial Times: 1620-1689.* HarperCollins, 2004

Raum, Elizabeth. *The Dreadful, Smelly Colonies: The Disgusting Details About Life in Colonial America.* Fact Finders, 2011.

Websites

Due to the changing nature of Internet links, PowerKids Press has developed an online list of websites related to the subject of this book. This site is updated regularly. Please use this link to access the list: **www.powerkidslinks.com/ahac/colo**

Index